THINGS
I NEED TO HEAR

THINGS
I NEED TO HEAR

AUSTIN BARRY

CONTENTS

❂

Dedicated

To each arrow
And every archer
And to all the times I've found myself
Late again, for yet another sky.

❂

And with gratitude

For the Pretenders, and the Offenders,
the vandals, the outlaws, and the Zimmermans
Who have held my heart throughout.

❂

"I'll see God in everything, in trees and pain and nights in spring,
so why do I still long for a home?"
—Zach Bryan

"I beg you, to have patience with everything unresolved in your heart
and to try to love the questions themselves as if they were locked rooms
or books written in a very foreign language. Don't search for answers
that could not be given to you now, because you would not be able
to live them. And the point is to live everything. Live the questions now.
Perhaps then, someday far in the future, you will gradually,
without even knowing it, live your way into the answer."
—Ranier Maria Rilke

Prologue

Words; the kind poured forth from hearts bereft and bleeding, and cast from raw hands like tiny melodies across oceans of paper, have always been a kind of salve for my heart. They are little messages, captured and corked into bottles and thrown out upon unrelenting tides, washing up on even the most barren shores of our most deserted islands, showing us a glimmer of a wholeness that lives beyond the many veils of our doubt and despair and dismemberment. These requiems of cadence and consonants and vowels, humming life into all the things that feel like dying, become like the song to which the soldier yokes his stance, so that he might continue forth, into all the battles he was never meant to win.

Yesterday was my 37th birthday, and each year beckons the reclamation that our brokenness is not meant simply for the purpose of being repaired. That we are not here to epoxy ourselves back together by any means necessary. That, in fact, we fix ourselves at our own peril, because the wound is not only the place through which the light enters us; it is also the portal through which that within us pours forth. It is the way we become carved open enough, so that the intrinsic and the elemental which resides behind our carefully curated and conditional I's and Me's and Mine's, can emerge undaunted and touch it's own face in the all that surrounds. This sacred dismembering is the doorway through which we must walk when we are, as Dylan says, tired of ourselves and all of our creations. And it is only through this divine intimacy that we come to know the love that lives, hiding behind the barbed wire peripheries of our war torn hearts and anguished minds. And it is distributed not in spite of our brokenness, but because of it. Breaking has never been the problem. It is the fixing that kills us.

They say that it is our responsibility to be the change we wish to see in this world. As such, it would follow that, sometimes we must also say the things we need to hear. And so here are things I need to hear. In defense of being and brokenness, and the fatal recollection that it is not our job to fix what we find in ourselves or in each other. Our work is, quite simply, to breath it and, god forbid, to love it.

Consider This

Just consider this:
Consider how many seemingly separate things
must come together
in order for any one
thing to occur at all.

Just think of it:

Of how an entire cosmos has been architected
and moved through the primordial pulse
of being and nonbeing
again
and again
and again for millennia

So that you can sit right here.
Right now.
Perhaps in anguish.
Maybe in ecstasy.
Maybe at H&R Block,
getting your damn taxes done.

But consider neither your state
nor your preferences for
or against it.

Simply consider this:

Consider that the animating principal has made you an instrument
through which creation might play out its song, and that the genesis

of The Instrument That Is You is the result of billions of stars, spiraling
through infinite space, igniting in flame and then imploding back into
the Void; over and over and over again, just so that this
one
breath could sing through the delicate flute of your windpipe.
Right
Now.

How many encounters? Missed connections? How many collisions?
How many cigarettes smoked to how many songs played on repeat?
How many tears shed from how many eyes throughout how many
generations of humanity?

How many canticles sung by how many crows have echoed through
how many empty autumn branches? How many blood red leaves
have swirled to the melodies of those avian songs, through how many
molecules of atmosphere, on their way back down to be reclaimed by
the same soil from which they once rose?

How many stars devoured by how many black holes?

How many beams from how many suns have carved
through the immeasurable darknesses
to bring this moment to you?

Just precisely how many things
have had to happen
so that you can breath
this
one
breath?

More than we could ever hope to count, beloved.
So many more than we could ever hope to count.
And yet still, somehow, we wonder:

Is this enough?
Am I enough?
What must I do? To make it feel like enough?

And so then how might we sit? How might we relate to the place from which we hear this incomprehensible song? And how do we wish to offer our voices to the eternal hymn of being? How might the way in which we play the Instrument of Our Embodiment change, were we to consider that universes have been created and destroyed, over and over and over again, so that this moment can merely exist? So that we can be together right now? What would it mean to consider this?

It might mean gathering our trust within times of darkness and destruction. It might mean becoming enamored with that which we have assured ourselves is utterly mundane. It might mean prostrating to those moments of perceived stagnation, no matter that they fall short of the external metrics by which we gauge value and measure purpose. It might mean that moonlight through a window, etching its monochromatic shadows over a silent wall, could be its own, inimitable masterpiece, worthy of your entire love.

And so, beloveds, what would our song be then? If we knew that in order for us to be here, wherever that is *right now*, an entire universe had to come into being? What might our song be then?

This gift of which we take part, has been billions upon billions of years in the making. Galaxies have had to be born so that we can ride together on subway cars avoiding eye contact
and drink tea at night by crackling fires

and hide how terribly misplaced we all feel
and smile when we pass a dog on the sidewalk.

If we were to consider all of this, then perhaps even an afternoon at H&R Block couldn't dull the unique and unrepeatable magic of being alive.

Feeling Meta

This.

This here.

This is the place in which our spiritual barrage has always been
doomed to fail.

Where the bullets assigned to mangle our sense of separateness fall to
the ground in expiration.

Where the blood we pledged to spill in the name of The Great
Remembering runs dry.

This is where our altruistic assault on the prodigal delusion falls short.

This here.

This is the doorway through which we are not meant to walk.

The threshold upon which we will remain dwellers.

Where the inherent homesickness seeded within the soil of our
humanness takes its stark and quiet stand as something of which we
were never meant to fully rid ourselves.

How could it be?

Once, we felt it all. So much so that we could not stand.
Then we traded the grips of sensation for the vast perspective of Meta.
Oh how composed we became then. How absent and easeful we were.

But this?

This place, in which we feel everything, and yet remain unpossessed by the specters of such palpable sensations.

This place, in which we are submerged in the flood of each wave, but where we cannot drown; where we are both present and absent, all at once.

This place here, weeping as we watch the dancers twirl across the stage, not part of their choreography, but moved no less than their bodies, as simple witness to their exquisite grace. Moved by their mangled feet, hiding inside perfect satin shoes.

Who can meet us here, in this place both within and without? Who can sit in this place with us now? A part of all things, and yet wholly apart.

First we think, only God. Only God knows what this is like; this divine Self-remembering, only realized through the relentless odyssey of self-forgetting.

Then we remember, and mothers too! Mothers know what it is like to live inside the cells of another being and yet to exist, somehow, completely severed from them.

And then we realize that children, too, know the pain of such parting; know the dull ache of this ancient memory of wholeness, echoing inside every pulse of the body that has carried them away from that first place of unperforated belonging.

And lovers know this ache; of hearts beating in the names of both service and sovereignty; of the struggle between the need to be separate and the need to be one.

And all breathing bodies know the divine intimacy of this separation. They are reminded with the song of each breath. Reminded when the air surrounding the lungs momentarily becomes an integral part of what makes us, and then again when the exhale pours forth into the vast terrain of "Out There" and "Not Me," separate again, and yet still, somehow essential to the mystery of you and I.

And gradually we come to recognize that there is not one embodiment of Spirit, in the vast landscape of all that is, that does not know the exquisite ache of this mystic dissolution. That there will never be one breath taken, that does not sing the song of this intimate connection between that which separates us, and the enduring ties which bind us to the all. That there is a sundering required to embark on the embodied journey, and yet even in the wake of such dismemberment, still something luminous endures. Something which carries with it the soft memory of a wholeness, too illusive for us to inhabit fully, and too innate to ever really be taken away.

And then we rest inside of our unwavering efforts, finding a new sort of belonging in this place where homesickness takes to its throne upon the heart of the human condition.

In this place, where envelopment and dismemberment dance together to the drum of a rebellious heart beat.

In this place, where the inevitable failure of our efforts to transcend the Holy Rupture becomes the most authentic expression of what we are.

And the ache of our longing, while no less palpable, is no longer a problem, but rather the purest expression of our immutable home inside the original pulse of creation, and a humble incantation, sung from every fiber of our being,

To the place from which we came,
To the place to which we will return,
To the place from which we never really left at all.

The Altar is the Apple Tree

It is true that the world will unveil her heart
in the moment of your stillness.

That simply your presence is her invitation to disrobe
and stand unencumbered in the glow of your attention.

This is true.

But it takes t i m e .

Time spent in stillness.

You must sit, for many mornings, in the luminous pink shade
of the apple tree while she blooms.

You must arrive, over and over again, as she bares and drops
her fruit to the ground.

You must witness her each dawn, as the last star fades
from the horizon.

Watch as she turns to gold and renounces her offerings
of beauty and fruit and shade.

You must be with her, sunrise after sunrise, while she sits
in her own sort of stillness, branches empty of sap
and thick with white
iridescent snow.

It takes time,

And many cycles,

To begin to know something.

So we arrive, again and again, breathing in and out, each morning in
stillness at her altar, only to discover
that her mystery was never meant to be solved.

Merely lived.

Simply Felt.

Always loved.

And recognized in t i m e.

Loving Cup

To that Love with which we long to merge
we must arrive with a commensurate desire to be torn to pieces

From whichever loving cup we choose to drink
in pursuit of our inalienable wholeness
when we accept the sacrament
we resign ourselves to dismemberment

Because if we place ourselves on Love's pyretic altar
in the name of becoming whole again
and if when we arrive
the words that roll like dew drops from our wet and parted lips say to Love
Make me whole again, but please, don't tear me apart
Well then we have neglected Love's only condition

Which is simply that we relinquish our form
at the foot of any one of its myriad demonstrations
That we would bring with us only a willingness to break character for
and to be broken by Love

That we would recall how each breath and every act is nothing more or less
than an embodiment of, and a prayer back, to that Love

And so we come to Love in wholeness, and we come to Love in pieces
And we come to Love to be remembered, and promptly taken apart again
And we come to Love to find that there is no place where Love is not
And we offer Love all that we have, the sacred and the broken
And we take all that is given, the holy and the profane
And we allow ourselves to be ravaged by Love's every offering
However tender, however vile

Because the Sea of Love harbors no preference
For any one of its waves
And if we wish to arrive
To be polished by its waters
To anoint our brows with its spray and our tongues with its salt
Then the simple requirement rests sweetly
in our unequivocal willingness to be utterly devoured
To be irreparably vanquished

Love make me whole is but one part of our serenade
Love take me apart, is the other.

To All the Love I Never Knew

For every word that wasn't meant
For every tear that fell unmet
For all the lies that I believed
And every breath I gave away
For all my youth and moments wasted
The faith poured into a godless room
And the heart whose armor was forced open
Only to find itself, beating alone
Choking on the candy coated nothings
of a goddamn lonely love

There need not be a drop of bad blood
As it was only through cutting myself apart for the other
that I became revealed to myself

One anguished layer at a time
Shedding paper thin sheets of bone
Like pulling blood from a stone
Until there was nothing left to hide behind
Until I took myself apart enough
to witness my own shame
And the river of my self-disdain
Pouring forth from a heart cracked wide
Ambushed by every hurt I had ever known
Drowning in the flood of no less than every pain I had ever hidden

For this exalted dismemberment, I have only all my love
For that which we refuse to feel, we will never have the chance to heal
And so it had to be the love left lonely, living like a flame upon the water
That would become the sledgehammer, taken to every wall I had ever built

And the longer it stands
The heavier it is
And the heavier it is
The harder it falls
And the harder it falls
The more that it hurts
And when at last it came down
I was left with nothing
Save the guttural reckoning
Of how very little I had mattered

I've grieved broken leather
and frayed laces and worn out soles
For longer than he felt my absence
The one for who'm I threw myself away
Affirming my worthlessness without hesitation
As quick and as easy to exchange as a pair of old shoes
And my instinct to make it sweet again, at all my own expenses
Showing me that I concurred

And therein lay my shame

For we accept the love we believe we are worth
And when we spend our heart's currencies
On those who use us for their own gain
Simply to protect themselves from their own pain
And who welcome our open veins
Merely to paint the dull shadows upon the walls of their caves
Who will illuminate and boast our names
But will never be brave enough to meet us in the dark
For those who confuse their oldest wounds
For the freshest of stabs
Bestowed from our loving hands rubbed raw

From tending lacerations for which we were blamed
But did not place
We either find another
To take us in and reaffirm our fictions
Or let love break absolutely everything that we are not
So that, one day, we might have something real to give

And we let the light left over from a heart on fire
Illuminate the hallowed truth
Of how little we must have thought of ourselves
To acquiesce all that we had to one who thought naught of us
And dare to call it love

And we are faced with so much self-contempt
For playing such a monstrous fool
For living in such squalor for so long
For believing we could only ever be good for so much nothing
That our blood was worth no more than a temporary adornment
Upon the hollow heart of a stranger
And hidden beneath all our childlike questions
How could they? Why would they?

Is the only one that matters
*How dare we expect another to value that which we ourselves have
    deemed worthless?*
And the humble recognition
That this question was never theirs to answer
This pain was never theirs to fix
That this work was never theirs to do

But where once I drowned in shame and folly
Only gratitude remains
From the depths of a heart forced open

And rearranged by disregard and brokenness
A heart that drums me forth into being now
Worth the work of breaking down
Worth the work of welcoming the Void
Worth the work of rebuilding
And worth the love of one who knows
That the word is not a word at all
But a body in motion
And a lifetime of days and nights spent tending
Worth the work of a love that, when tested in fire
Does not simply melt

And so now, my hips and my thighs
And all my breathless nights
Can finally belong to another
Who knows just what to do with every one of them
Who need not boast my name, but arms strong enough
And a heart bold enough
To hold all of it
Never because tomorrow is promised
And always in the face of looming loss

Because there is not one thing we get
That we do not have to give back
Not one breath we take
That will not be surrendered
Not one beat of a heart
That will not return to stillness

And so this manner of tending demanded by love
Is not the sort that stokes the flame of its own masquerade
In a futile evasion of an inescapable loss

It is a caring akin to the way we tend the seed
Ready and willing to burst through the walls of its own encasement
And pour itself faithfully down
Into the darkness of an underground
Knowing nothing of light
Delighting in the death of everything that it is not
So that it can welcome its own becoming

And so to all the love I never knew
I have nothing left
Except to thank you
The only thing wasted
Was all the time spent believing that it was.

Grace

Grace is defined as "unmerited divine assistance given to humans for their regeneration or sanctification."

Where there is impenetrable righteousness, there can be no grace. Despite the wholehearted nature of our searching, we will never find grace in the land of incessant perfection and perpetual goodness. Its defining characteristic is that it is bestowed, irrespective of merit or worthiness. Its magic is in its unconditionality and its portal is our fallibility.

So when we periodically become snagged on the sharpest edges of our humanity, and when our focus becomes enveloped in the transcendence of folly, perhaps we could learn to pause, and to soften the rigid tensions of these self-imposed narratives, steeped in the toxic brew of our perfectionism.

Excellence is ego's ideal endgame. Grace, on the other hand, is magic.

The gift of grace does not arrive in spite of our blunders. Rather it comes *through* them. It requires our folly, and all our woeful humanness in order to exist at all.

The mind strives for an unattainable quality of perfection, while the heart simply aches in the quietude of its deepest knowing, for grace.

And it is precisely when we falter; when our carefully curated efforts have all come up short; when all our time spent appears wasted; when every intention has fallen flat and there is not even a breeze left with which to animate the sail of our purpose; it is precisely at this moment, when there is nothing left in our arsenal of polished offerings, through which grace makes its entrance.

The gifts of grace are immeasurable, but perhaps its greatest mercy is its capacity to illuminate a wholeness, to reveal and restore us to an enough-ness, constantly sought while all the while sitting quietly within. Its power is in its capacity to turn us toward the exquisite intimacy of this moment, wherein our breath is distilled through the agency of our wretchedness, and is finally unmasked as sacred amongst all of our eclectic and highly choreographed manners of bromidic self and banal prayer. It is felt when we recognize that every expression of the animating principal is sacred, and that this one breath is easily as sanctified as our most effusive expression of worship on parade.

As long as we are human, as long as we continue to be disheveled and flawed, we will know grace. So forget your perfect and untainted offerings of self, for it is only from between the cracks in your facade through which grace will arrive. And wrapped within the gossamer of this mercy is the sacred remembering that your presence is your prayer. That your breath is your vocation. That your offering is quite simply your heart. And in the glow of this knowing, all things become sacred. And we are invited to receive and to treat them as such, so that this deluge of mercy might emanate indiscriminately forth from within us, with the same natural cadence and instinctual repetition as this breath in our lungs, right, now.

Venom

I watched it
Like a red star, with a tail as long as the sky
Falling through the night
Exquisite and uncertain
Like nothing I had ever seen before

I waited for the impact that never came
Rather it disappeared silently into the night
Leaving nothing behind, save an empty sky
I guess it wasn't what I thought
Just another case of mistaken identity

For some of us, evading impact is not our soul's prerogative
We lack the savvy for guarding against the shattering that surrounds a
    falling star
And we have no talent for self-preservation at the expense of others
No instinct to protect ourselves from pain at any cost

You were so like the politicians you claimed to loath
Pretending to stand for others
All the while tending only agendas born of your dread
I don't think you know what it means to die for something
That to give yourself up for another
Does not demand that we cease our pulse in their name
(if only it were so easy)
But that we arrive with a willingness to dismantle every part of
    ourselves that yields to the fear
So that we can love truly, and for free

Sex with you was always scripted and sad
And still I stayed
Alone in the dark, pretending
Keeping so small, that I was barely even there at all
Keeping myself quiet and tame enough to fit in your pocket
So that you might never have to acknowledge
Your weak heart and your hollow bones and your trembling hands

But it is no act of love
To protect a beloved from their pain and their faithlessness
To deny them the corrosive agency of heartache and despair
And it's foolish to indict another for the ties we bind round ourselves
And when finally I collapsed beneath the weight of your façade
And could deny you your emptiness not a moment longer
After all your big talk of love
And your free flowing blame
In no time at all
You had left me for dead

Fortunately
There are many ways to dispose of the carnage left behind
After the mutiny of a counterfeit love
Some bury their dead and walk on
Others burn what's left behind and anoint their hearts with the cinders
You neglected even to retrieve the ashes
As if the Grace left mangled and bleeding in the street were so easy to replace
She need not warrant a second a glance
Nor a moment to sit tenderly with the searing stillness of her absence
As if she had never existed at all
And so you welcomed another with ease of a Sunny day
And so it goes

But some of us do not simply forget
Some of us adorn our necks with what's been lost
Leaving her bones to glitter at the base of our throats
Drumming the anguish of her absence into the walls of our heaving chests
Chipping away at the collarbones caging our hearts
Like falling water through granite

And we cut off all our hair
And start running up mountains
Forcing hot blood through weary veins
Begging our broken hearts forward
Until our knees scream and our lungs bleed
Until we can escape the face that lurks out the corner of our eye
Until we can promise never to abandon ourselves like that again
That we will never again mistake a clowns cheap trick
For magic

I've heard that heartbreak is a long black limousine
Mine appears to have child locks
But I know that only the meek
Measure the value of love
Using the metric of security
By how much of it they might harvest
From the presence of arbitrary, interchangeable others

But the simple truth
Is that you could not recognize the difference
Between a heart racing for fear of loss
With one in love

And while I will always be enamored
With the man I mistook you for
You are not him

And I would rather die, loving like an outlaw
Than live as a beard for a man who cannot face himself
And awake to a set of eyes in morning light
Wishing that they belonged to someone else.

On Decay

When you see the sun, shining bright through yellow leaves, igniting the tops of the trees, and you feel your heart ache and catch fire with the beauty of it all, what you are relishing in is little more than decay illuminated. Your mind will tell you that decay is not beautiful. That unmaking is a bitter end. But your heart will show you otherwise. And as the leaves of preference begin to drop from the branches of your being, your mind will be the last thing to let go and yield to the ancient wisdom of the heart.

The mind tells us that wholeness lives primarily in the summer branches, sagging with their ripe plums, swollen with sweet juices, dripping with abundance and the promise of satiation. But the heart will show us that it is no less attendant in that moment, when the leaves turn golden and drop to the earth, anointing our eyes with their beauty, perfuming our noses with their fragrant demise and blessing our hearts, with a knowing much deeper than any proclivity to which we might instinctually cling. But the tyrant between your ears will also insist that anything of value must surrender easily to measurement. Like pounds of ripe fruit in a basket, as opposed to the simple, luscious drizzle of nectar that traces your chin in the wake of your first bite. *It's only the heart which knows the stark difference between the metric, and the value it has been assigned to represent.*

The mind is the last thing to submit to that which the heart has learned from the simple experience of its own aliveness; from the wisdom harvested of its own, rhythmic pulse, echoing some 100,000 odd times a day, from within the prison of your collar bones. And in order so that our preferences might stay protected from the havoc wreaked by contentment, any knowings of use or of substance are obliged to sneak through the cracks in our cerebral fortresses, so that our nimble little minds can't reason them into corners where they can be kept small and easily wrangled. And since there is no way to separate any one part of our knowing from any other, we can trust, well beyond the many shadows of our doubt, that anything we allow to raise the tides of our current level of consciousness, will invariably lift and anchor all of that which makes us. Because the One is found in every single corner of the many. As such, we might entertain the possibility that, even in the absence of an instrument capable of measuring our gains, our returns may in fact be multiples of our efforts, and far further reaching than we have the mental capacity to entertain.

So, do not submit to the prison of your preferences. Because the wholeness we crave is not found in any one part of the cycle of things, but rather in the entirety of the cycle itself. It must be sought after in the emptiness as much as it is in the full. It exists, not simply wrapped within the exclusive splendor of the revelation, but inside of the seeking itself. And it's felt in the heart when the two dance together, cheek to cheek on the head of a pin, spinning through an immeasurable ocean of space, stepping in time with the rebellious beating of the primordial drum. The allure of our preference for a singular sway in the dance, or a particular expression within the cycle, is simply the barricade we build between ourselves and our immutable home inside this vast cosmic arrangement.

So might we behold the golden leaf, as luminous as it is brittle, in its final expression of light and of color, with the same sort of reverence we bring to that fresh and ripened plum? Could we come to value the empty branch with the same regard we reserve for the one which is full? Could we learn to hold ourselves with reverence for all that transpires within us, even when we are void of any measurable offering? Even when we are becoming undone and unmade, could we be willing to illuminate, with the simple instrument of our most tender acknowledgement, the decay that inspires leaves to burst into vibrant flame as they spiral down to rest in and feed the earth, with the same generosity of spirit we give forth to new buds, coiling out from their deepest slumber and toward the rising curve of springs warmest invitation?

We must. Because until we cease our futile attempts at stagnation in favor of preference, we will remain banished in exile. The wholeness we seek is not simply found in the fullness at the top of the inhale; but rather throughout the entirety of the breath cycle itself. And our home in this world exists in ever-present unconditionality, as soon we choose to worship at the trembling temple of the heart, and to take our wisdom from the cyclical journeys of breath and of pulse. The mind will always prioritize its preferences, and as such, these somatic insights we accumulate through the devastating privilege of being alive, are not for nothing. In fact, they do not even require our conscious acknowledgment in order to move us further up the spiral of our own conscious capacity. It is through the portal of this moment, the one in which emptiness ceases to be the nemesis of that which is full, wherein we become, like golden leaves returning to the earth, re-membered within the cycle of things. It is only here, in this place, where we find that home from which we could never be bereaved.

A Prayer for the Dying

(to Cosette, with love)

This morning you lay by my altar.

While I looked up prayers for the dying.

Most of them were for forgiveness
and courage and faith and grace.

But you need no forgiveness
because you have never in your life wrought harm.

And the courage you had
to come here and watch over me as you did
and the faith it must have taken
to place yourself in the care of one so flawed
so that I could be blessed enough to be kept in yours
would make it entirely tone deaf
for me to pray you either courage or faith in your final hours.

And as for grace?

If one defines grace as unmerited divine assistance
then from the day we met
without a moment's exception
you have been nothing less than grace incarnate to me.

You have been my unmerited divine assistance
from day one.

And so while I pray for you now
as you lay dying at my side

fading away
like even the brightest constellation will
against the sun
all I can bear is to ask the Lord of Lords
that you be welcomed back
with the ease of one so deserving.

That your return be as dignified and as graceful
as you always have been.

And to say thank you to the Divine Maker
from the bottom of my broken heart
for appointing you as my guardian
and for entrusting my care to you for this last decade and a half.

And so I sit here with you now
with nothing to offer you on your journey.

Except tears.
Each one its own prismatic vessel
for grief, and love, and gratitude
for all of it.

Even this.

And while I pray you ease through the labor of this transition
I will pray myself the forgiveness, and courage, and faith and grace
(they say are to be reserved for the dying during this most sacred moment)
as I prepare to walk in this world of the living
without you at my side.

Light Loves Brokenness

Light loves brokenness

Adores brokenness

Longs for brokenness

Light lives for the sundering

It comes alive at the moment of rupture

Dancing through the shattered labyrinth of form

Like a distant voice through the immense carving of a canyon

Echoing the sound of the original severance

A shrieking through stone cut wide open

Light merely touches the surface of that which is too whole

It rebounds off any exterior too polished or smooth

Recoils from that which is too solid or well sealed

But have you seen the sunlight erupting through shattered water?

Have you watched it explode through the unsaleable fracture in your
        windshield,
as the rays blasted through the brokenness
you keep meaning to get fixed?

Light enters through crumbling walls and cracked hearts,
through quintessentially damaged New Mexican windshields
and wishes unmade and dreams left undone

It arrives through the spaces between

Through the places in which we were not met
Where we were left repugnantly vulnerable
and overexposed

And so we hold our breath until we are blue,
anything to avoid breaking the abating calm
of the surface

Goading ourselves on with this deluded tale of a destiny,
waiting somewhere beyond the horizons
of mending and repair

Driven forth by this insatiable appetite for repurposed loss,
to fill the void with whatever material we can,
anything to make it feel better

And we dress the carnage left behind,
by dashed hope and vile heartache,
with whatever bandages we can find

Faster than the speed of light, we bind the flesh back together,
sabotaging the very salvation we've sought through such tending

And we cement the vacancies left in the wake of our latest loss and
repurpose the pain as best we are able

And we find comfort in our renovation
because *anything* is better
than brokenness

Make it useful

Spin the straw into gold

Purge the discontent and the longing from your heart

Tame the fish and calm the seas

Anything to keep the water intact

But light loves brokenness

Adores brokenness

Longs for your brokenness

Light lives for the sundering

And have you seen how it erupts
through the mangled surface of morning waters?

How it dances through the fractured calm,
nearly blinding in all its luminous glory?

Have you seen it?

Yes, light is only made brighter by brokenness

Thank God we have not yet managed to tame the fish.

On Disruption

And here we sit.

Equilibrium expired, despite our best intentions to acquire an impermeable brand of unflappable composure. Perhaps we've already been consumed, yet again, by an especially electric squall of devastating humanness. We might be dangling our feet over the edge of a rocks glass, or a resolution, or a new lover, or a next ambition, or whatever it is that promises to banish this un-enchanted version of ourselves to the unmarked grave in which we are so certain it belongs. And so we trudge forth into the new year with our shovels and our torches of declaration, prepared to entomb anything that dares detract from our composure.

From where did these inveterate monuments to perfection originate? The ones declaring, with such confident authority, that the only tolerable way to be, is poised? That we must orient ourselves toward an incessant ascension of mythic proportion, always on top of the wave, always in favor of evicting those messy and precarious facets of our humanness? When did we decide that uninterrupted stasis and smooth seas are our most prized possessions? Our most noble of aspirations? The North Star toward which all of our best intentions must steer? When did we start speaking of disruption as our nemesis? Was it the morning we began to flee from our own shadows? Perhaps it was the same day we decided that our vision for equilibrium is our best ally, and our mission to maintain it our most imperative assignment.

But holidays can be such a disruption.

And these early winter sunsets are such a disruption.

Weather can be such a disruption.

And to love is a disruption.

And to loose is such a devastating disruption.

And not being able to predict each day, down to the minute, is such a disruption.

And fatigue, and hunger, and fullness, and restlessness, and sickness and rage are all such disruptions.

And being seen in a moment of need is such a disruption.

To need is a disruption.

And storming the fortresses guarding our conditional notions of self and of worth, so that we might recall the wisdom, that all our noble studies of what is right and what is wrong, are brittle and lifeless as sun bleached bones lying breathless in the sand, is such an overwhelming disruption.

And to be alive is perhaps the fiercest and most rebellious disruption of all; as it unapologetically refuses the interminable perfection from which it came, in favor of that which is bitter, and flawed, and destined, by design, to expire.

And perhaps contentment too, is its own radical sort of disruption; asking us to dismantle our never ending agendas, for the sake of simply existing within the imperfect and yet entirely complete fabric of one moment.

And so we come to recognize that disruption is not an inconvenience blocking the path.

Disruption *is* the path.

And of course, with those early winter sunsets, comes that rose golden hue at the tops of the trees as the sun disappears from a cotton candy sky.

And there is that perfect softening at the center of the heart, when we are witnessed in the flood of our many frailties, and every fiber of our being insists that we must hide. But, for once, we don't. And when we are revealed in that moment of intolerable vulnerability, that is the power of love recognized. That is the perfect center enveloped within the myriad stories about what we need to do better, so that we might learn to corral and evade disruption.

And then we come to recall, that the purpose of the resolution is not to help us evade disruption at all costs, but rather to position ourselves so that we might learn to welcome it at each and every turn. Because it is precisely that which we are so sure requires fixing, that we must learn to hold sweetly, even in the absence of repair, (just as it is that which we feel so urgently needs to be preserved, that we must be willing to have dismantled). And while we are rarely inclined to hold a knife against the throat of self preservation, we can rest assured that surrendering to life's innate capacity to wreak havoc on our plans, will ensure that we are not left to stagnate inside the prison our preferred versions of self.

And so we are invited to recall, again and again, that the balance we so desperately seek is not a perfect state of equilibrium, but rather a constant recalibration around an unwavering center. And often it is the very disruption we are so keen to avoid; the one from which we will do anything to protect ourselves, that obliges a shift in our gaze toward a more resilient center, that will not be dictated by something as fickle and uninformed as our individual pallets or misguided notions of how it should be.

And so, here you sit, equilibrium expired, despite all of your most valiant efforts. Consumed again by your instinctual commitment to the storm of your own transformation; a creature at the edge of the old world, ready and willing to be dismantled and recalibrated; trusting that your next point of balance will arrive in the wake of yet another, looming disruption, that will strip away another layer of that which is not really you, so that you might shine with a brilliance you have not yet dared to imagine.

And to share yourself in that moment of prismatic vulnerability, is a gift to each and every soul, who has forgotten that the language of love can be jagged and dark. That transformation is itself, an overwhelming disturbance of an old, expiring version of identity. It is a brave and generous reminder that speaks directly to the primordial wisdom, housed in the most ancient room of the heart, that rests in a knowing, with neither doubt nor despair, that God is as much the demagogue as the architect. So let the winds blow and the earth quake and the waves swell. And if you should feel called to wait until the disruptions have all been controlled, the polishing completed and the balance perfected, in order to share yourself or sip the soma of contentment, only know that you will be waiting forever.

Permission

(ode to Olivia)

The sun pours itself over the horizon this morning, rays unfurling
to the rhythm of a relentless drum.

Hail has a habit of roaring in behind the soft warmth
of a late April bloom.

Abrupt. Shocking. Disrespectful.

At first, your bones seek shelter
from the assault of a cascading cold
Reverberating down the nape of your neck
spilling down
between the blades of your goose pimpled shoulders.

And then, gradually, this storm of uninvited spring hail
becomes permission.

Permission, cloaked in dark grey and cold
pounding water.

Cold enough to hold in your palm.

Solid enough to dent the roof of your car.

Slowly, it comes, with each new, unapologetic crash
of ice on the window.

Like hoof beats, clattering
over slick cobblestone.

The permission to bring forth the wildest, most unexpected parts of yourself.

The permission to disregard the daffodils,
pretty maids that they are,
all in a row,
planted with such care.

That relentless drumming on the roof is your permission
to be arduous in your entirety,

And to delight in the unwelcome harshness
of your innate and intrinsic wholeness.

Hyperbolic Love

I don't want to hear about the bullets you'd take
And the veins you would open
Of the deaths you would welcome
Or the railroad tracks upon which you'd surrender your head in my name

All these Anythings you would allegedly do
I want none of them

You don't have to tell me that moonlight on my skin
Is all you will ever need
And I'll never ask you to starve yourself
Or to save me from my time when it comes
Or to catch an imaginary grenade just to prove your heart

Even when they splinter my insides like shrapnel
All I ever want are your truths

The only work I would ask of you
Is that you disarm the many devices of your fear
And slow the train of your reactionary ways
And learn to steer
That you would awaken to your own pain
And begin to dress and cauterize the wounds
Gushing hot blame
And rushing you to terror

Love is not measured through flagrant claims
Of what one would do in the event of unlikely and imagined scenarios
Love is boots on the ground
It is grit and grace and gold
It is humble as dirt and noble as stars

I never needed your hyperbole
Just your calloused hands and your crooked smile
Your battered heart and your broken teeth
Just for you to recognize yourself enough
To see what I was not

You asked me to live inside the broken home of your hyperbolic love
Where despite the many Anythings promised, nothing was delivered
And from the seductive boudoir of the martyr
You might still claim that you gave your all
And though you would have fought any army out there, just for me
Your everything was never enough for my fickle heart

But I never needed you to battle the enemies outside
Only the ones within
Because from you, all I ever wanted
Was a heart strong enough to hold all of me inside of it.

To Be a Good Home

And today, I am a vessel for longing.

A chalice for grief.

A refuge for questions destined to remain unanswered,

and stones left forever unturned.

So I will do my best to be a good host.

To be a welcoming home for such despair.

Because it is not I who lives Life, but Life who lives me.

And the only choice, is to breathe all that is given.

So today, I will be a sanctuary for this longing bestowed within me.

Today, I will not bear this anguished heart as a burden, but rather hold it like a prayer, and tend the richness of its ache, until it comes to lay, like blood soaked marigolds, upon the boundless altar of That which moves it all.

And I pray that I might be like the hollow reed; that I might become like an instrument, tuned simply to harmonize with the immutable sanctity of Life's myriad expressions; resonant enough to siphon it's celestial melodies through the mangled landscape of a desolate heart beneath a darkened sky.

For it is not I who lives Life, but Life who lives me.

And so today I will do my best, to bet a worthy host for even the most harrowing expressions of such hallowed, infinite, Source.

The Divine Rupture

There is an aching; a sharpness that hides inside the heart, carving into the ancient cave walls of the chest when we are moved in just such a way. This pain is part of our embodied inheritance. It is a nod to the place from which we came. And we spend so much of ourselves trying in vain to refuse the endowment. This pain is as fundamental to our humanness as the heart that beats in our chests; we cannot cease it without ceasing ourselves.

Sometimes the ache lies dormant. Quiet and dull. So still and so small that we may even forget that it is there at all.

But if we watch closely, we will see that it always returns. Or, perhaps, that we always return to it. No matter how diligently we practice, or how positively we frame our circumstances, and irrespective of how pious we become or how many trigger points we transcend, we are tethered back to this pain.

It is the echo of the original severance; the one which brought us forth into being. For the original sin was not a sin at all, but a wound. A separation. A Oneness, which stirred and severed itself into many pieces, and then scattered itself throughout the interminable vastness of the new cosmic arrangement.

We were told that a woman bit into an apple so that she might know of the world.

But in the beginning, there was no woman to want; no apple to bite.

There was only This. And it stirred and perforated itself so that it could partake of its own love. So that it could know and love itself in every way. So that it could hold its own grit inside the same, soft and open palm that holds flecks of gold up to catch the light. So that it could glisten and bleed at the same time, in its unwavering commitment to the karmic assignment.

There was a great dismembering then. And we feel it when the broken shards of our most sacred pasts etches the story of our separation into the walls of the heart. Like cave paintings drawn in blood; remembering our selves back to our Selves, back to each other, over and over again, until there is no self, and no other left to remember at all.

You cannot run from the stone inside your shoe.
From the blister on your heal.
From the wound that all we share, left over from this Divine Rupture,
echoing, over and over and over again,
with the perseverance of a beating heart
drumming the exquisite anguish of its own separation forth into the world.

This stone, this rawness, this wound, is our invitation to pause.
To touch the most sacred heart of our humanness.
To connect back to the original wound.
So that we might remember, even if just for a moment, that we can never be fully severed from that which we most elementally are.

So do not run.
Your pain is your invitation,
To be as still as you have ever been.
And when, eventually you begin to move again, it is not away from, but towards.
This pain is your invitation to follow the red river, pouring forth from your mangled heart.
Like a coyote choir, chasing the sun over the curvature of a horizon, bloodied by its own, exalted descent.

So that you might remember, through the felt acknowledgement of your dismemberment, that every river is just an expression of, and a highway back to the sea.

Trust Everything

The green light you missed, as much as the one you made
The timing that was all wrong
The dream that slipped through your fingers, like sand through the
wide open aperture of an oversized hour glass
Trust the death that sits like a raven, just behind the perch of your left
    shoulder
The grief that forced the breath from your lungs and your brow to
    earth
And all the roses that failed to bloom this year

Trust the rain that did not fall
And the sun that refused to shine
Your dry mouth
Your cracked lips
Trust your broken heart, and the shadows you have misdiagnosed as
    light's nemesis
Trust the moonless sky and the empty winter branches
Trust the vacancy you feel, churning within the substratum of your
    most abandoned self

Trust Everything.

In your cowardice as much as your courage
In the dynamism of your own ignorance
In that which is uncertain, erratic and unpredictable
Trust in the course that you cannot, despite your best efforts and
    instruments, chart
Trust in your emptiness
Trust in your defeats
In the abominations of your faithlessness and your doubt

In all that has taken you apart and anguished your heart and
	terrorized your mind
and left you bereft of all your precious knowing
Trust in your deepest despair and your discontent
In your perfect longing
Trust in your questions as well as you do your answers

Trust that there is no thing here that does not belong
No place where God is not
No experience that is not an integral part of the karmic assignment
No thread and no space between that is not essential to the cosmic loom
and its interminable weave
Trust that there is nothing here unworthy of your entire love.

Trust the mountain

Trust the mess

Just, Trust, Everything.

Where Are You?

Right now,

Where are you?

Are you here?
Here with us?
Held, here, within the unrelenting embrace embodiment
and all its brokenness?

Where are you, right now?

Are you here?
Or do you reside within the serpentine prison of your skull
Mistaking atomic shadows for bars
Consumed by the burden of your myriad tales
Absorbed in a habitual manner of fantasy
One that you know all too well
is all too ready
with the simple ease of a melody
to devolve into a nightmare?

Where are you dear?

Weathering the storm of your own mind?
Alone inside your head?

Come back.
Please come back.

You want to live in the world darling, not inside your head.

You want to live here,
where the warmth of the nearest star on your skin welcomes you back,
An invitation from ninety some million miles away
begging you back
to this ground
right here
beneath your own
still breathing
body.

You are so much more than your mind, darling.
So much more than your thoughts.

All these worries
about all that you fear
you will not have strength enough to carry
So much squandered upon innumerable untold things
that are sure to break you.

But from Here, beloved,
the terror of your perceived inadequacy yields to the truth
That you are already carrying it!
And that it has not broken you
But has taken you apart
just enough to let the light in
and to grow something unabashedly
new and previously unknowable.

Four legs and soft brown eyes
Crimson petals, persevering
amongst parched, red earth and formidable spines
The prismatic tear, tracing down
the perfect curve of your cheek

The primordial drum
of your very own heart
All beseeching your return.

Even the stone inside your shoe
The thorn drawing blood from your side
The piece of your heart cut away
Still longing, like a phantom limb, to be returned
All of it welcomes you back, beloved
All of it welcomes you back.

Today, the warmth is that brilliant star, kissing your open palm
     through the mouth of dawns first light.

Tomorrow it may be sourced of your own hot blood, pooling inside
     the sanctity of that very same reservoir.

But the invitation is always the same:

Come back, beloved, come back
Do not exile yourself in the wilderness of thought
Live here, in the world, with us, sweet one
Not alone, inside your head.

Civilian Love

There is little less inspiring than a love
Cut like paper snowflakes with safety scissors
And tied with string to the windows of a house adorned in tinsel and
    fool's gold
A glittering attempt to refute any hauntings and deny any dark corners
So that as long as the earth beneath never moves
And as long as the sun above always shines
Its ghosts and its fractures might consent to remain unexamined
And it will masquerade as something of value

This is the home of Civilian Love
Where counterfeit heroes, void of courage, hide from their shadows
    and evade the rain
So that their painted faces never run, and their soft bellies never risk
    evisceration
It's where the pacifist, dressed in samurai drag
Spends his life making and fixing the masks he shows to the world, in
    place of his actual face

Civilian Love is a darling idol at best
Sterile and tame, toothless and declawed
A house cat in a lion's mane
It is a false god, dripping in pedestrian rosaries and idle prayers to the
    Lord of Self-Preservation

As such, Civilian Love can satiate only a Civilian Lover
And there is little I desire less, than a Civilian Lover

Who has never been in love at all
Though he speaks the word each time he drowns himself inside a new
    set of Ocean Eyes

And his unwavering belief in his own lie assures him, every time, that
it is true
He is devout in his delusions
A con artist, falling for his own deceptions
And from the decorated windows of his eloquent and untouchable
façade
He cannot see that the words he speaks are void of currency
And that mere belief will never be enough to engender truth

The Civilian Lover fucks like his whole existence is fraud
Like he is desperate to escape himself
Frenzied to evade a pain he has neither capacity nor courage enough
to acknowledge
Even with his hands around your throat and his hip bones pressed
against your own
It's like neither one of you are even there at all
And the Civilian Lover won't realize that you faked it every time
And since he's never cared enough to know his own mind
Or to concede the depths of his own heart, even to himself
And since the thing he calls love is little more than an instinctual
artifice
Devised to hide him from himself, and himself from the other
And the person with whom he effects his singular objective always
falls second in line to the objective itself
He will never have to know the fallacy of his Great Casanovan Charade

It's neither malice, nor ill will which spurs him forth, and he is
certainly not void of care
He simply has never had the courage to give life to love's sacred name
To take up his sword and animate his many flagrant claims with the
sanctity of action

Instead, when he is frightened, he simply finds something that scares
him less

And when he is plagued by his weakness, he simply surrounds himself
    with whatever returns to him the illusion of his strength

But to resent the Civilian Lover is as cold and as useless as resenting two
    eyes for their color blindness
For he knows only tinsel and fools gold and snow flakes cut from colored
    paper
And no matter the sincerity of his effort, he will never forge a sword,
sharp enough for loving, from colored paper

No, I will never again entertain a Civilian Lover
I want to be disarmed and gutted by Love
For what is its purpose if not to take us apart?
And to shine its light on the parts of ourselves left previously undisclosed?
To ransack the vault inside which we've imprisoned our hearts
And ravage all of our precious mythologies
And cut the throats of our pleading bedtime whispers of *please don't break
    me, please stay tame*

I don't want my love to guard the gates
But rather to storm the fortress and rob me of my many fables and rub my
    skin raw of all its impeccably painted layers
And touch my Original Face
To leave nothing left standing between I and I
So that there can be nothing left standing between It and I
And nothing left standing between You and I

And so I have little interest
In Civilian Love
With Civilian Lovers

Who will go on mistaking ephemeral moments of relief from their long list
    of intolerable fears

For Love's sacred ground

Because what is love's purpose if not to dismember our facades again
and again?

To make known the hauntings and the cellars and the darkest corners
of mind and heart?

Imploring us through it's magnetic mystery to turn toward all of that
which we have told ourselves we simply cannot face

So that we might become brighter and braver and more daring than
ever before

And the Civilian Lover can only endure a love which promises to
protect him from all this audacity

One that never asks of him to face himself and to assume his, as of
yet, immaterial integrity

And so, for those of us who wish to go rogue

Who long to trade in our civilian clothing

And become Savages for Love

We will have to abide by a new code

One that states quite simply:

If we can stand to lose it

And if it is not sharp enough to run us through

Then we don't want it at all.

Interminable Love

What to do with an interminable love?

Spend your time wishing it were not so?

Delegate your attentions toward trying to kill that which you know
will not die?

Domesticate such unruly devotion with your mind and its myriad
rationales?

Or perhaps find mercy in a tragic sort of gratitude.
Is there any aspiration more exquisite than to be possessed by a heart
that can love without end?

Is this not what you prayed for, every morning,
hours before dawns first light, through tired eyes
and thick resentments and a weary heart?

That you might simply become an instrument of love and devotion,
no matter the cost?

That the entire vessel of your being could become animated
by a manner of love demanding no measurable reciprocity?

A kind of love that pours forth for free,
far beyond the meritocracy of mind and matter?

Be careful what you wish for.

Pray at your own risk.

Interminable love, is not for the faint of heart.

And so the faint of heart, will never have to know its ache.

And the interminable lover, will always run the risk,

Of loving alone.

And so, mercy to the ones who barter with broken hearts.

And mercy to the fools
who sought warmth and reprieve
in a love without end.

For absence is its own, barbarous manner of presence.
And interminable love was never meant for those unwilling
to weather the sadistic scope of its storms.

Two Birds

(anti-venom)

We were like two birds
Caged, right next to one another
We did not know that there was any other way to be
We knew nothing of flying
Nor of wind
Nothing of sun
Only the reflection of a light left unexplored
Illuminating the delicate, golden bars
Which kept us from ourselves
And from each other
For we had never learned how to be birds without cages

And so we kept our doors shut
And our wings gently folded
And used only our softest, indoor voices
Terrified that all we could ever have was each other
And only so long as we stayed quiet and small and tame
Only so long as we surrendered to entrapment
Behind luminous, golden bars

We dared not open up the doors
And learn to stretch our wings
And to turn our heads
And tune our gazes to distant horizons
And outrageous possibilities
And to sing our songs in unapologetic outdoor voices
Because we did not yet know
How to be birds without cages

Until suddenly I could not stand to watch our wings atrophy another
    instant
Could endure not another song,
caught and wasted forever in the backs of our throats
Could no longer gaze through golden bars
and all the vacant space   between

And I felt the stirring of life inside the empty shell of my heart
It was the most sacred impulse
It wreaked of uncertainty
It screamed of death
And I lusted to see you trust your own wings
And for you to know the unique beauty of your, as of yet, unsung melody
So that we could learn to be birds free of cages
So that we become something
Real for ourselves
In order to become something real
For each other

And the only thing greater than the fear
Would our wings even work?
Is there even such a thing as a bird in flight?
Or a love without bars?
Was the despair
Pouring forth in audible whispers from the recesses of my heart
That we would never know the closeness for which I yearned
Without opening our doors
And that two birds who consent to their cages
Are resigned to a commensurate manner of love

And the songs you had sung to me
In the warmth of the kitchen
Where food was plentiful

And the future certain
And delicate, golden bars
Protected us from ever drifting too far
Or getting too   close
Songs of secret gardens and feathered Indians
And Tennessee whisky and love undying
Assured me that we were like swans
Bonded for life
Through ice storms and relentless winds
Through bullets flying and moonless river crossings
That the only thing we needed
In order to become for each other
Was to learn how
To become for ourselves

But I misunderstood the nature of it all
That to you, all swans appear the same
That to you, I could have been any body
That my cage just happened to be the one closest to yours
In that particular corner of that particular kitchen
At that particular moment in time
That I just happened to be there, that's all
I had not understood
That you did not want to become for anyone
That you simply needed someone, anyone
To protect you from having
To become for yourself

But it was precisely that unrequited love for you
And the childlike faith in who I believed you were
And in what I thought we could be
That demanded the doors be thrown open
For flight has always been our birthright

And so I thank you for your words void of currency
And for your barren and listless love
For your uninspired heart and all your recycled sentiments

And I thank you, above all
For the songs I have learned to sing
And for the trusted wings now spread wide
For the heart that, through this pain, has learned pardon
And for the gift of an incomprehensible aliveness
I never could have known
Flying alongside a bird who fears his own hollow bones
against the menacing uncertainty of the open sky

In the beginning, I loved you so much
That I consented to be caged
And in the end, I loved you so much
That I demanded we break free
And when I saw that your love was little more
Than fool's gold and last call promises
I loved myself so much
That I will never again allow golden bars
to take the place of proper sunshine
For birds with no faith in the mystery
And no allegiance to the sky
Will never know freedom

And hearts that bend for fear
Will always break in the face of love.

You Are The Moon

It seems that wholeness is considered one of our most aspirational trophies. As such it is hunted by the masses with an exhaustingly dutiful sense of commitment. We track wholeness through dry deserts and dense forests, seeking it in our chosen disciplines, practices, palatable experiences and communities, and by becoming so engrossed in our day to day existences that our lives become fuller than we are reasonably able to sustain. And yet somehow, we are still empty. We ransack our lovers in search of wholeness. We long to recognize it in the eyes of our children. Or we ignore the stark feeling of our separateness all together, through these same mechanisms and more. And we do our best to evade the very Pause which holds the key to our salvation, and instead trade in the silence for a labyrinth of chatter.

Sometimes we pursue a path toward self-betterment with a notion that this illusive wholeness lies somewhere, gracefully perched in uninterrupted equilibrium, on the other side of our accomplishments; somewhere beyond a certain number in our bank accounts, or hours spent meditating, or a welcome acknowledgement of our hard earned successes or inherent specialness. We imagine that if we were only able to transcend our humanness enough, with all its limitations and perceived imperfections, that we might attain this manner of illusive enlightenment. And thus we strive for it. We go to church, to the bar, to the mountain, to the sea, to the mat, hoping to find it in any of these places. And eventually, after lifetimes of failure, we are forced to brave the stillness and to sit silently and bow our heads at the mysterious altar of our insatiable wanting, waiting for enlightenment, for wholeness, to descend upon us and into the darkest and most reprehensible recesses of our being.

But it's all in vain.

No matter our righteousness. Regardless of our commitment. Irrespective of the natures of our devotions.

It will always be in vain.

The wholeness of the moon is not dependent upon our perception of her in the sky. It has nothing to do with the sun, or with the position of the earth. It has nothing to do with her luminous performance or her capacity to ensorcel our heart strings in her late autumn glow. Most of the time, our lunar spotlight is shrouded in shadow, (in our shadow no less). However, her fragmentation is little more than a cheap facade at best. And as the astronomical gurus of history have shown us, the moon is no less whole when she appears as little more than an echo, of a sliver, in front of a bright blue sky, than she is when she rises in full illumination, flooding the darkened landscape with her gentle defiance. No matter her placement in the sky, she animates lovers and tides alike, as her magic is not confined to her light.

We are akin to the moon in the ever-present truth of our wholeness. It has nothing to do with our deeds or with our convictions, or with the ways in which we orient ourselves within our lives. *(Right alignment might permit us to recognize our truest nature, but it is not responsible for creating it).* The wholeness we so dutifully seek is unattainable, simply because it is always right here. We starve for it, and yet here it is, a feast simply awaiting our acknowledgment. As such, we cannot attain enlightenment, or piece ourselves together in wholeness, but rather we must recognize its constant presence. Our practices, our communities, our dedicated exertions toward evolving versions of ourselves, might allow us to strip away at the veils which shroud our elemental entirety, and at best they will help us to orient skillfully in the presence of this truth, but we must beware our natural tendencies toward striving in the name of this discovery. Because the harder we work to attain something that is already an inherent part of our being, the further away it begins to feel. To seek, is to imply an absence, and this wholeness we crave, is anything but.

We are simply the moon; always whole, despite the shadows periodically painting an interpretive image of fragmentation.

So breathe like the moon and remember. In the felt acknowledgment that your wholeness is not found in a lung filled with air; but rather inside the entirety of the breath cycle itself, remember. Your emptiness has never been the enemy of your entirety.

Remember, my friend, even when you are as dark and as empty as a sky without a moon, your wholeness cannot been taken from you. No matter that you feel little more than a waning sliver in an unforgiving sky; you are as exhaustive in your darkness, as you are in full illumination.

Recognize yourself.

Forget, because you're human, and then remember again.

What Does It Matter?

How to behold the unequivocal rawness of a human experience?
With its interminable demands, repetitive plot lines and transient
shapes; always infused with expiration and dripping in paradox;
how do we assign meaning to an experience so fleeting? When
that which we carry is so often brimming with tears and imbued
with the dull ache of our desolation in the wake of such a
discernible separateness? When we know that nothing we
could ever make will ever be built to last, but always promised
to break, how do we infuse each step with resolve?
Each drum of the heart with vocation?
Why does any of it matter?

Because our lives are simply waves, and the sensations we experience
ripples, all expressing directly from the unobstructed ocean of Source.

And an opportunity to acknowledge the wave, and to hold it with
daring gratitude and fierce compassion, is also an opportunity to
acknowledge the divine sea from which it was made.

And so, whatever it is, that connects us with presence to our lives in a
given moment, is sacred. And in bowing to that momentary expression
of Spirit, we bow to the God from which it was made.

Even when the ripples drawing us into our respective realities, are
grief, aloneness, misunderstanding, or the stark recognition that
we have spent so much of our short time, living a simple life of
elaborate illusion; that which is present, is our most direct line back
to the Animating Principle. And so we need not be ashamed of our
venomous thoughts or resist our own toxicity. Anti-venom demands
a touch of the original poison in order to heal the afflicted, and the

salvation we seek from our sickness is shrouded within even the most unceremonious expressions of our humanity. When that which consumes us is one of the lesser narratives at best; whatever the thread, weaving us through this experience of being, yoking us to this place in which we sit or slump or laugh or weep or lie breathless today; it is unquestionably sacred.

Sacred, explicitly because of its intimate and unrepeatable subjectivity.

Sacred because of its immovable authenticity.

And it is precisely when we are able to welcome what is, that we permit ourselves to come home. Because what is here, now, is our tether to this world. And though ultimately we will transcend it, until we do, this world is our tether back to Source. And so for now, worldliness is our direct highway to the Godliness we so diligently seek.

And when we recognize the elemental truth of all this perceived chaos, when we remember the homecoming that lives, within even the most banal and wretched of human experience, we find that in fact, each moment of our lives is consecrated. We find that every drum of even the most broken and labored of hearts, is without doubt, sanctified. And we feel, in the enduring iron infusing the momentary rush of hot blood through tangled veins, that we are no less than what we have always been:

Expressions of infinite Source.

Dancing in light.

Waltzing through dark.

At once beating hearts and bloody fists.

Kissing in cars and throwing stones at glass houses.

Baptized in each other's tears, to a hymn wept beneath the soft invitation of a glowing moon and held, always, by the relentless memory of flickering lights, cascading across a ceaseless expanse of darkened sky.

Inviting us to return in prostration to the ultimate paradox of the embodied experience; the inescapable truth that that which we contain, is immeasurably vaster than the container which holds it.

May we all, of our own patience, and in the triumph of our
own time, come to know that each and every moment of
our lives is a simple celebration of Spirit. That each wave
of experience harbors the same amount of God as every other.
That we are merely the Formless, frolicking in form's masquerade;
so that our humanness might be further illuminated by our
deepest knowing, and less burdened by the many shadows
of our finely detailed despairs.

The Work of Loving

The Pain
It does not go away
And all the everythings we use
And the doomed crusades we endure
And the many walls we erect
To protect ourselves from its assault
Simply serve to hold it in
And barricade the highway promising our return
To that sanctuary we seek inside ourselves,
And each other

With every wall we build
To stave off The Pain
We make of ourselves refugees
Who blame the lovers
And the myriad others
For never feeling quite enough
Like the home for which we yearn

And so we set up tents in the periphery of ourselves
For this barren wasteland is all we have
And every time the wind blows we fear that it's the end
And so, homeless, we must seek out kinder climates
Because by playing the futile game of denying The Pain
We have denied ourselves
Of all that is whole and rich
And true and powerful within

So pack up your tent if you must
And go seek your perfect weather

But I ain't goin nowhere
I will prefer to cut myself apart
And rearrange the pieces
To blast it all to dust
So that I might live
Closer to that place
In which all of this shows itself
For what it always has been

Our stunning lostness in the labyrinth of mind and matter
Our confused ways of loving each other
Nothing more than God on Hallows Eve
And sunlight streaming through broken window panes

Because without admission to that
Which seeds itself within the heart
We have no currency anyway
So go sell what's left of your soul
And try to purchase a day promising no storm
I'll be here praying for the lightning
Bring me the dynamite
Let life do away with me
As I have made her

We are not what we have built
We are not all that we have spent our lives making
And the work of loving
This work of recognizing ourselves
Is not the work of building up
It is the faithful labor of breaking down

Because who we are lies in wait
Behind all these things that we are not

It is a manner of coming undone
The mess of unmaking
This is the work
Of loving

And if it is not worth our brokenness,
Then it does not have our love
And in the midnight of your deepest despair
In the sacred mess of your unmaking
Know that you are in the work of love
And in the solstice of your darkest night
In the abysmal pain of your undoing
Trust that the value of the lessons learned
Is worth so much more
Than the cost of all your time spent
Courting a light you are unwilling to let it in.

No Matter What

There are but few storms which can compare
with the ones which ravage daily the shorelines of a human heart
and wail, without relent, against the cave walls of a human skull.

And so when faced with the mythic swells of an anguished heart
and the unremitting currents of a mind in turmoil
it might serve us to recall
that a Courageous Heart
is simply one
which welcomes everything.

And that a Wise Mind
is simply one
which knows when to leave itself behind.

And that the ever present invitation of the human adventure
implores us quite simply
to harvest the wisdom we so desperately need
from the pain we so faithfully encounter.

This is how we spin straw into gold and turn water to wine.
This is how we tend the ravaged shorelines of the heart.
This is how we swim through even the most merciless of tides.
This, and only this, is how we come to love each other,

No Matter What.

Austin Barry, 2024